from Lincoln
February 1977

DANCE

Portrait in pastel of M.L.E. Moreau de Saint-Méry by James Sharples. The Metropolitan Museum of Art, Bequest of Charles Allen Munn, 1924.

DANCE

An Article drawn from the work by M. L. E. MOREAU DE ST.-MÉRY entitled: REPERTORY OF COLONIAL INFORMATION, compiled alphabetically (1796)

TRANSLATED, AND WITH AN INTRODUCTION BY LILY AND BAIRD HASTINGS (1976)

A DANCE HORIZONS PUBLICATION

Copyright © 1975 by Dance Horizons

All rights reserved. No part of this book may be reproduced or utilized in any form or by any means, electronic or mechanical, including photocopying, recording or by any information storage and retrieval system, without permission in writing from the Publisher.

International Standard Book Number 0-87127-062-5

Library of Congress Catalog Card Number 75-9157

Printed in the United States of America

Dance Horizons, 1801 East 26th Street,
Brooklyn, N.Y. 11229

Introduction

Médéric Louis Elie Moreau de Saint-Méry (Martinique, 1750 - Paris, 1819) was a brilliant member of a venerable French family whose ability, curiosity, and energy led him into a number of fruitful activities. He was influential enough to hold several governmental positions, to count Tallyrand among his best friends, and to have his portrait made by Edmé Quénedey (1756-1830), a French artist remembered for his likenesses of Mozart, Méhul, Kreutzer, Rousseau, and Madame de Staël.

Moreau de Saint-Méry's interests in the dance, in social history, and in manners are brought together in what is believed to be the earliest surviving book on the dance to be printed in the United States. It is here published complete in English for the first time, translated from a copy lent by the Yale University Library.

Dance was first issued in 1796 in Philadelphia, printed by the bookseller-author at the corner of Front and Walnut streets, where Moreau de Saint-Méry lived during some of the most violent years of the revolutionary period in France. As the title page to his book states, this "article" is part of a much larger work devoted to the culture of the "Colonies," a work which apparently never reached the typesetter, though the manuscript still exists. His powers of observation are considerable.

Dance is concise, very readable, and frequently profound. It provided the text, if not the inspiration, for quite a bit of Blasis' much more widely circulated and famous publication, *The Code of Terpsichore*—as Lillian Moore has shown in her informative piece in Volume 5, Number 10 of *Dance Index* (that admirable review edited by Lincoln Kirstein, 1941-1948); for fuller background on Moreau de Saint-Méry, a discussion of his dance aesthetics, as well as specific practices in Haiti, the reader is referred to *Dance Index*.

Lily and Baird Hastings

Publisher's Note: Lily and Baird Hastings have attempted to maintain the flavor and style of Moreau de Saint-Méry's prose in their translation. Likewise the typography and format of this edition approximate as closely as practicable that of the original book.

Facing page: Title page of Moreau de Saint-Méry's
Danse. The Beinecke Rare Book and Manuscript
Library, Yale University.

DANSE.
ARTICLE
EXTRAIT D'UN OUVRAGE

De M. L. E. Moreau de St-Mery.

Ayant pour titre: *Répertoire des Notions Coloniales.*

Par ordre Alphabétique.

A PHILADELPHIE,

Imprimé par l'Auteur, Imprimeur-Libraire, au coin de Front & de Walnut streets, N° 84.

1796.

DEDICATED

TO THE CREOLES.

By their Admirer

MOREAU DE SAINT-MÉRY.

AVERTISSEMENT.

WHEN this paper was read before certain literary societies of Paris, the several reports released were so incorrect and even disfigured that the author believed it was his duty to publish it unabridged as he had composed it in 1789.

It is one of a number of articles making up a kind of *Colonial Encyclopedia,* undertaken with the aim of familiarizing Europe with the nature of the colonies, presenting the subjects in an order which would facilitate and simplify re-

AVERTISEMENT.

searches, also often comparing the colonies with each other.

My use of the title *Repertory of Colonial Information* resulted from my belief that one man would be foolhardy if he tried to produce a truly encyclopedic work, and from my desire to challenge more knowledgeable pens to perfect and also correct whatever I had produced.

A number of different obstacles prevent the completion of this plan at this time.

M. DE ST.-M.

DANCE.

ARTICLE

Extract from the Repertory of Colonial Information, *alphabetically arranged (*).*

IT would be absolutely ridiculous to attempt to discover the origin of the dance, because that would be to infer a different origin from other important manifesta-

---

(*)This article was written early in 1789.

tions of the soul, all of which belong to the passions. Actually, anyone who feels an emotion strongly will express it by movements very similar to dance; and, if this joyful emotion is felt by several individuals, it is natural that hands and arms come together almost involuntarily in a manner which links one to the other, and the movements mingle and are shared.

Of course there is an immense gulf between this expression of joy by primitive men and the voluptuous graces of civilized people; but one can easily see that, as in many other matters, all art is based on natural laws.

In spite of the tumult and the confusion resulting when a number of individuals unite in joyful emotions, if their movements take the form of the dance (even the most rudimentary) a sort of simultaneous and ensemble character develops which seems to lead them in an orderly way. The proof is found in the round dance, necessarily a primitive one since it is really a *danse champêtre*, which is shared by people possessing the highest degree of civilization—as one can observe among the modern Greeks. In the round dance each person is part of the circle, each one sees all the others, and the chain which is formed by the arms becomes the governor of all the dancers' movements.

One can realize that, if the number of participants is too large and the dance is not the result of a sudden emotion, but rather the expression of a gay memory or a means of finding release in pleasure, in place of the bizarre and dissonant cries of the crowd verging on delirium, the accents of a few would predominate. Then one notices how one singer gives the dance a unity, and a dominating voice takes precedence in such a way that sooner or later it inspires new techniques, as one learns that flexibility of the voice is preferable to the outbursts of untutored throats.

That great teacher, Love, must also have counseled that the melodious voice of a shepherdess would add to one's pleasure. Eventually the discovery of musical instruments enabled the dance to exhibit charms which were hitherto unknown, by making it more animated, and enlarging its form; then the plaintive Syrinx, by means of the burning lips of Pan, brought new sensations to the soul, and new sources of voluptuousness.

Through the spectacle of the unfolding centuries we are able to understand the progress of the dance. And we can observe and realize how dances were transformed by different peoples and different classes of the same people; one can note the pure joy of peasants expressed in circle dances to the strains of a musette or a violin in movements which make no effort to mirror the enchanting magic of Guimard, Saulnier, Miller, d'Auberval, Vestris, Gardel, Théodore, Nivelon, or Laborie, whose sophisticated ballets are directed by the graces.

Interpreters of former days used to perform dances which took on characteristics appropriate to the persons they were depicting or to events they were remembering. On occasion, solemn or lively, sometimes chaste, and at other times frightening, they depicted either the quality or the tastes of a people.

Through the medium of the dance, in pleasurable anticipation, the warrior could nourish his soul with feelings, carrying him toward a glorious reward: such as the smile which a Spartan maiden would bestow on her soon-to-be-victorious hero. A great deed was thus reproduced before an assembled crowd, and the love of country was evoked within the frame of the senses as one swore to live and die for her. What a powerful way to imbue men with courage, to make them benefactors of their country, when they are brave enough to let themselves become the vessel—these dances enable the triumphant protagonist to enjoy the depiction of his heroic actions, as the frightful aspects of war disappear before the seductive qualities of victory.

There have been no religions which have not adopted characteristic dances to preserve and expand their faith, or to maintain the notion of their ancient origins; and the memory of the famous dances performed in honor of Bacchus is still with us. Even among the early Christians, on certain special days and at certain periods, joined by the priests, the faithful held hands, dancing a round in the church with lovely, timid virgins whose humble mien and innocent charms expressed nature's greatest beauty.

Dances among civilized peoples are subject to capricious taste, as are almost all other manifestations of their customs, whereas among savage or untutored peoples (to use the expression which the pompous use), dances retain their forms virtually unchanged. Just as a greater number of ideas offers the possibility of more combinations, variety of every sort indicates a people is more advanced—perhaps the dance could serve as an indicator of the degree of civilization. For example, it is clear that in an existence in which almost the total occupation of the day is devoted to obtaining the necessities of life, the atmosphere is not favorable to progress in the dance.

Nevertheless, this rule is not absolute because progress in the dance also depends on the climate and the nature of the nourishment of each people.

In areas which are extremely cold, nature has created people capable of fighting constantly against this cold and its concomitants. As they are obliged to hibernate, so to speak, for long periods of time, and forced by the winds and all the vagaries of the weather to live practically without communicating among themselves, they assume something of the wild ferocity of the animals from whom they steal their clothing. In a word, men in these rigorous climes have plenty of strength, but strength coarsens one's manners, and, if it does not extinguish sensibility, at least it lessens the delicate sensations of voluptuousness. Certainly the dance, daughter of pleasure, would not dare to be seen in the middle of virtually eternal ice and snow.

In temperate climes, however,

the seasonal renascence of fair weather always excites people with a secret longing which seems to promise a new existence. The horizon clears, blue skies return, the earth recalls its verdure, fields begin to shine, and the air seems to cure our ills—everywhere nature is sweet and fair as the brilliant colors are unveiled—everything has a soul which is open to pleasure. Thus youth, happy in its inexperience, comes to join in the dance, and to enjoy the delicious charms which can best be enjoyed by innocents.

On the other hand, there are

peoples for whom this awakening of all which breathes is largely lost; they are peoples who, living only by hunting and by fishing, must consider rest as real pleasure—for they experience and enjoy only difficult and useful activities. But wherever man is a shepherd or a farmer, his gentle soul is open to pleasureable impressions, and, whatever his station, he is favorable to the dance and ready to welcome Spring as the smiling visible tableau of the period of inspiration.

It is only in cities, where all pleasures seem contrived, that Win-

Dance. 15

ter is the season of the dance. The tastes are so extreme that simple joys give way to luxuriant follies found in balls which lack gaiety. The real joys are to be found at modest balls. Nevertheless one may regret that nature takes on mourning for such an extended period. One can hardly believe that the memory of its attractive quality can inspire such abandon at the springtime renewal; however the countryside does enjoy this monopoly. The beauties of our cities, too systematized or too frail to enjoy pleasure which they do not control, would think they became too rustic if they enjoyed the same season as peasants, for generally their celebrations exhibit an exaggerated sense of self pride.

But above all it would seem that the dance was created for the lands with sunny climates. Everywhere dance is a pleasure; there it becomes a passion. The blood, which is practically always warm, contains the germ of all voluptuousness, and in their fleeting lives the southern peoples aim at enjoying every minute. One observes that the land workers love the dance best of all. Pleasure is a food which they enjoy particularly. Always changing, for them nature is constantly varied; quickly rich and prodigal, it favors them, and, since they seem not to live as long as the people of frigid lands, they fear to lose a single moment.

My observations concerning the dance and climate, the habits and customs of peoples, are easy to verify, and I will give examples based on my studies of America.

One does not find vivid motions in the dance of northern America. The Eskimo, shivering under his fur coat, spends his entire time amassing a sufficient supply of food to eat during the snowy season. And the northern-most people are even less likely to find pleasure in the dance than the Eskimos—for they are hardly touched by the warm rays of the sun, which seems to avoid them for long periods of time. This fate is common to practically all the inhabitants of the far north: the Laplander will never be noted as a lover of the dance.

However, as one considers the peoples located between 50 degrees latitude and the tropics, one finds a number who are devoted to the dance, depending on their particular climate, their customs, and their food. I am not only speaking of Europeans who have transported their tastes to the New World, but also of the natives. Specifically, the savages of Canada, of Mississippi, and many others in this vast continent, sometimes turn to the dance—one can observe the proud Natchez, the wild Algonquin, and even the furor of certain tribes of ancient Virginia who let their joy be found in the celebration of human sacrifice. Thus, each people bares its soul in the dance, and the very diversity of which I have been speaking shows its origin to be as I have stated. But whereas some dances are caused by the ferocity of the participants, other savages who obtain their food from their work on the land turn to sweeter pleasures of a milder nature. For them the dance offers relaxation, and, when they are not involved in the atrocities of fighting, they express themselves in a manner totally different from their warlike customs.

A general observation is that all untutored peoples living between the 25th and 50th parallels have dances which are sad and monotonous. Beating a drum and singing tunes resembling the psalmody are their only inspiration for movement, characterized as they are by strength and satire alone. And the insatiable cupidity of Europeans has brought an immoderate taste for strong liquors to these peoples, whose passions have become even more lugubrious, and the source of combats, quarrels, and differences.

Now if we consider the inhabitants of the tropics, we will find them charmed by the dance to which they abandon themselves with voluptuousness because it is quite true that the local temperature and their life-style influences all aspects of their characters. Guiana well illustrates this point—hunting Indians are scarcely disposed to the dance, which would be for them an additional fatigue, while farmer types love the dance and count it among their most cherished pleasures.

Thus on every side we find confirmed the fact that the dance is a kind of exhaltation which affects people continuously and directly, depending on the star of the day: people abandon themselves to it without reservation, and when they tire their desire to continue awaits only their renewal of energy in order that they can repeat the same joyful experiences.

Further proof of the influence of climate on the dances of the American colonies is evident when one compares their dances with those found in various European metropolises.

Changing tastes and fashions are as important here as in the respective capitals: for instance in the French colonies the Minuet had its day, and then the Contradance in the form of Rigaudon or Allemande. For a while the Anglaise received all the votes. Later one had to know how to waltz and execute *jetés-battus* or else give up any pretention of maintaining one's reputation as a dancer. In this climate there is a vivacious and prolonged passion for the dance, an ardor in seeking to satisfy this passion, and a fear of missing even one opportunity of indulging in this pleasure.

At a ball the Creoles take on a different aspect from their langorous bearing which causes one to judge indolence as their dominating characteristic. All their movements are gracefully naive and touching, while their animated glances betray incipient and developing voluptuousness. As they accelerate their delicate steps with a tempo Europeans would find difficult to follow, they appear to fear they cannot achieve the pleasure which seems to beckon them on. And one should not imagine that the heat provides any obstacle to the pleasure of the dance, the fires of climates become those of desire. Often one hears complaints at the shortness of the nights spent in dancing, and against the return of the sun which warns that at last one must rest. During the period between one ball and the next one often hears complaints that the waiting is intolerable, and would be unsupportable except for the attentive preparations made to ensure the brilliance of the forthcoming event with its plethora of new outfits. And exquisite taste ensures the success of the next event as everything which filmy dresses can do to increase the elegance of the ladies of tropical countries is called on to participate. Ah! as the art of pleasing is their greatest goal and gift, we must be grateful that they go to such great lengths to achieve their ideal, which in turn assures our own pleasure.

Who could possibly describe all

the emotions which follow each other and are mixed up in the heart of the young Creole, on whom nature seems to have lavished every quality to entrance her companions, when she arrives at the ball to become the focal point of the assemblage. An enchanting art has governed her entire appearance, and has served her all the better by hiding its triumph. Although every single flower and curl has been placed with forethought, one would think each placed by nature's fortune. She inspires voluptuousness, and her eyes which caress us are made up to embellish her charm in an innocent way. Her mirror has observed her beauty, but the praises she now receives are a thousand times as sweet.

The compliments multiply when the sound of the instruments gives birth to fresh temptations. A light step, a curved arm, a thin waist, and easily graceful movements reveal how dangerous she is. Gradually her face flushes, her eyes reflect the emotions of her soul, and she abandons a little of her precious timidity—all of which makes her even more beautiful.

Pleasure has endowed the

dance with a powerful charm. The hands which touch each other, the arms which entwine, operate like conductors of electricity producing an effect which is both certain and prompt. And how can one's sensibility not be affected by the delicious sensations which we feel? To begin with, the ears are profoundly touched by the sounds of the instruments; the eyes are flattered by the wide variety which fashion has made for them; the sense of smell is conquered by the variety of perfumes—and when all of these delights are seconded by the pleasures of the dance itself, their combination is virtually irresistible. How well love knows the power of these combinations, particularly within the empire of the ball, and how it practices with extraordinary success.

And how could it not be otherwise? This young belle whose prudent and severe mother has insisted that timidity is the quality of her sex, whose every inconsequential indiscretion will be pounced on, who has been protected against a thousand flattering overtures, is nonetheless brought to the ball apparently to undertake an experiment promising just the contrary. The dancing master has told her that one must smile at one's partner; he has instructed her in all the graceful attitudes which serve to stimulate one's imagination. Now her hand, that a man may not touch, is nonetheless touched and even held at the ball by a hand belonging to a happy partner. In the brief pauses of a Contradance the young lady cannot prevent her partner finding her charming, telling her so, and even repeating himself. I know that the hardy human spirit can defend itself, and escape many dangers—but what if the heart interferes and leads the spirit astray?

Ah! only if one has never danced with the object of one's affection can one ignore the force of this all too powerful magnetism. Few are those who must not credit a success to this pleasure where the soul is carried into a sort of delirium. Vainly do protective mothers and jealous husbands redouble their surveillance. Let them remember that wherever balls flourish the objects of their affection will inspire tender emotions and that one cannot always be insensible to the emotions one has inspired.

The influence of the dance is well known in the colonies, particularly among those countries where the carnival is celebrated with balls. One may say that when carnival time approaches one can expect some marriages; it has been proven that the project of many a marriage began at a ball. Perhaps one can even say that this is one of the reasons for the enthusiasm there is for the dance.

Here is my opportunity to cite a practice I have noted in several colonies, particularly Saint

Dominique: the practice of spending on dresses for the ball a sum which contrasts inappropriately with the fortune of the family. I know the aim is to increase the young lady's loveliness and to ensure the acquisition of a husband, yet I dare say that this zeal has perhaps repelled more than one prospect: a man of reason noting a penchant for luxury and expense which he might not be able to afford will resist and curb his amorous desires.

Realize if you will what a suitor must think when he observes the proud demoiselles, ridiculous to the point of changing toilettes five times in the same evening, and when he reflects how they would blush if one of their dresses had to be worn at a later ball. I am not reproaching the young Creoles themselves (whose coquettry is unduly attacked) but rather the parents who should think about those destined to become mothers of their own families though they are hardly inspired to become such when they are shown such futile, expensive ways of life.

In former days the pleasure of the dance was lessened by a kind of pride which had caused the invention of a code for all private balls. System and even research were necessary to determine who should open the ball and in what order each guest should dance his first Minuet. There was a master of ceremonies, sometimes several, whose functions were difficult, disagreeable, and even dangerous: difficult, because they had to survey constantly that the systematic code was observed; disagreeable, because it was virtually inevitable that some heiress would claim that she was forced to dance out of turn, *after* someone whose genealogy she recounted with critical comments, particularly if she was prettier than the one she criticized; dangerous, because the complaints fell on the master of ceremonies, who frequently was charged to keep out uninvited persons, or masqued persons, and in this region dance is such a passion (and one is not exempted from its susceptibilities) that it is difficult to accept refusal. Thus, more than one master of ceremonies has been obliged to put his life in danger in order to maintain the dignity of the position.

One day it was realized that a divertissement should not be a course of manners and behavior, and for a long time now, after the grandparents pretend to dance their Minuet and have embraced each other, the Contradances are arranged informally. It is up to the master and mistress of the household to see that every one enjoys the festivities. If a young lady is passed by, a considerate relative or a sensitive friend will do his duty by at least promenading the one who may not realize that lack of charm or grace is not admissible at a ball.

If one fears the ardor of the dancers may weaken, gradually the Contradances may be reduced—and either some older dancers perform the Minuet, providing variety through their participation, or else dancers who are capable of drawing applause for their brilliant steps, in spite of the severity by which one has grown to judge Minuets in recent years, will display their talents. When one observes that the dancers have lost all but their courage and the ladies speak of rest, this is a signal for Allemandes, Anglaises, and the Congo Minuet, and they spend several additional hours which are no less gay, and which pass very rapidly.

Finally, the evening draws to a close, and the dancer who took her place to begin the ball must leave because it is over. The "embracements" of the young people are accompanied by promises to find each other at the next ball, and each goes to his or her rest, happy and though tired, attractively flushed with the pleasure which has been enjoyed. Fortunate is the suitor who accompanies the object of his affection to her house, having found in the dance one of the most propitious inventions of love. Even more happily affected is he who finds passion in his soul, and after the ball is able to increase the pleasures he can taste with the lovely young Creole.

Sometimes passion for the dance can be harmful in climates where the nights are unpleasant, making it difficult to enjoy all ordinary pleasures of the ball; so in Saint Dominique, about 1780, they abandoned public evening balls in favor of balls called Redoutés, held twice weekly from five to nine in the evening. The pleasure is shorter but more frequent, and the mothers do not have the pretext that the fatigue of long nights prevents them from attending the balls. At the Redoutés of Cap-Français I have seen, among eighty young ladies, there were many who would have competed for choice even by a Sultan well informed concerning the perfection Mahomet is supposed to have reserved for him among the heavenly Houris.

In former days one enjoyed the dance more frequently because all one needed for a ball was a few instruments and the simple meeting of a few young persons. However, as luxurious toilettes extended their empire, or rather their impositions, these pleasant divertissements disappeared. Dancing has been reserved for sumptuous fetes, or public balls, where the spirit of particular groups of coteries was found and at which rivalries were formed and nourished—among a large company in which each faction kept to itself. Sociability and politeness have lost something in the process; one can see it particularly in the rather common scenes of the last days of the carnival, when the evening ball presents a display of masques, one of the main roles of which seems to provide opportunity for particular groups which have been formed on preceding evenings to criticize each other, and sometimes to complain bitterly of the wrongs a group believes it has endured from the others.

Without the restraint of reasonable persons, the dance would never stop in the warm season—as one can realize by observing the activities of those among the freed men and the slaves who do not practice this healthful moderation. One may consider this as a virtue among the colonizers—all of which leads to a two-part observation: first, that the national characteristics influence their actions—the English colonists dance less than the French, and the Spanish also dance more than the English; secondly, the native Creoles are more vigorous dancers than are the colonizing Europeans of the same nationality.

Freed men and their offspring are extremely fond of the dance. They follow the whites in their choice of dances, and in their manner of dress. Before they were freed the dance had a special charm for them, because it had not been permitted freely. (We know that difficulties often make a pleasure more spicy.)

In certain colonies, freed negresses dance only among themselves, for they are not admitted to other divertissements. It is not surprising that in places where the slightest nuance may manipulate to advantage, vanity in one's position is significant, and thus a mixture with white blood is indicative of certain advantages.

There is another point of pride which also has its curious side—that is, in those places where freed persons of various kinds associate with each other, as in some colonies, the different shades suffice to differentiate the classes, and there are balls where the freed ladies will dance only with white men, refusing to dance with men of their own color.

In order for the balls of colored ladies to be really attractive, these ladies should stop believing they are obliged to dress themselves exactly as the whites. Why cannot they observe that the same flower is not equally suitable for langorous blondes as for piquant brunettes, and that great contrasts call for careful preparations; why cannot they be coquettish characteristically in their own ways? Also, they should realize that approximation of movements is not imitation, and they must study the changes, the small steps and poses, which the graces have invented and which they alone can reproduce perfectly.

However, the participants dance for themselves; they are enchanted by the dance, for which they have an extraordinary aptitude. Such is the sureness of their ears, if they would only observe with care the rules of a teacher, they would easily become pupils perhaps unequalled by Europeans. They are beginning to realize this, for I know of rehearsals where instruction is given in order to unite the pleasures of the ball with those in being part of the human race no matter what one's color may be. Is it not pride which causes them to dress in taffeta for one ball, in chiffon for another, and in linen for a third?

Many slaves in domestic service in cities approach their white masters in their diversions; treated as they are in a manner which makes them feel close to the whites they begin to consider themselves as an intermediate class, between freed men and slaves, adopting many aspects of the whites. Thus, their dances, which they mostly perform among themselves, are the same except for certain piquant differences introduced as idiosyncracies. One who has attended their balls can attest to their individuality, and Callot and Teniers would have found much to paint if they had been able to see these grotesque performances.

When they resist their unfortunate tendency to imitate, negroes have charming dances, all their own, coming originally from Africa as they do; and the Creole negroes love their dances particularly, because they have performed them from earliest childhood.

The African peoples offer further proof of the passion these tropical inhabitants have for the dance, because they are sensitive to this pleasure with the same intensity they show for food and for life itself. Bloody, bellicose negroes on the Gold Coast are used to human sacrifice, and they perform ferocious dances typical of their nature. In the Congo, the Senegalese and other African farmers and shepherds love the dance as a relaxation and a source of voluptuousness. From all Africa, negroes who settle in French colonies with comparable climate continue their love for the dance—a love so strong that though exhausted by work they find the strength to dance, and even to walk several miles to and from the place of this delight.

When they are ready to dance, the negroes take two drums, that is two barrels of unequal length; one end of each remains open and the other is covered by a tightly stretched lamb skin. These drums (the shorter of which is called the Bamboula because often it is fashioned from a large bamboo which has been dug out) sound out as they are given fist and finger knocks by each player bent over his drum. The larger drum is struck slowly, while the smaller is used for very fast rhythms. These monotonous and low notes are accompanied by a number of Callebasses, containing gravel which is agitated by means of a long handle. The Banzas, a sort of primitive guitar with four strings, joins the concert, the timing being controlled by hand-clapping negresses standing in a large circle; the group forms a kind of chorus, replying to one or two principal singers whose remarkable voices repeat or improvise on a song.

A dancer and his partner, or a number of pairs of dancers, advance to the center and begin to dance, always as couples. This precise dance is based on a single step in which the performer advances successively each foot, then several times tapping heel and toe, as in the Anglaise. One sees evolutions and turns around the partner, who also turns and moves with the lady; while the

DANCE. 55

partner moves his arms with the elbows rather near the body and the hands practically closed, the lady holds the ends of a handkerchief which waves. Until one has seen this dance he can hardly realize how vivacious it is—animated, metrical, and graceful. The danseuses and dancers spell each other and the negroes enjoy the dances so thoroughly it is hard to bring them to a conclusion. These dances occur in open air fields where the land is smoothed out to spare the feet of the performers. They are named Kalendas, probably after the sound of the

Kalenda drum, which in turn may well derive its name from the Celt, Gal-ven-da, meaning *call them.*

In view of these elements it is clear that this simple primitive dance belongs to "uncivilized" people. The circular form, clapping hands, repeated songs, loud instruments, all indicate it to be an old African dance, performed by the Hottentots, and many other peoples.

In Saint Dominique, particularly in the western French part, there has long been known a dance called the Vaudoux, which requires two or four performers, and

DANCE. 57

which is characterized by movements in which the shoulders, head and upper torso move as springs. This dance is accompanied by the drum, clapping hands, and choral singing. I do not know the source of its name, but its effect on natives is such that sometimes they dance it until they drop, exhausted.

This is as nothing when compared to the Dance of Don Pedro, another negro dance known in the west of Saint Dominique since 1768. Don Pedro was a negro of Spanish ancestry, from the Petit-Goave section, who by his bravery and certain superstitious actions had a great influence on the negro population. Eventually he had to be arrested as a public incendiary.

The dance of this name, like the Vaudoux, is based on extremely vigorous movements of the head and shoulders, but to increase their violence the performers drink eau-de-vie which is mixed with finely pulverized gun powder. The effect of this drink combined with the vigorous movements has a great influence on the dancers, who enter into a kind of madness, with real convulsions.

They dance with contorted motions, falling into a kind of epilepsy which knocks them out and they seem near death.

It was necessary to prohibit the Don Pedro, because it caused great trouble and awakened ideas of violence contrary to public interest. The spectators, forming a kind of chorus, participate in the intoxication, and instead of becoming silent when the frenzy develops, they redouble the volume of their songs, increase the tempo, and aggravate the crisis in which they participate. How curious it is that man searches for his pleasure in such excesses.

The Creoles have adopted another exotic production which, also coming from Africa, had an even greater influence than any of the negro dances of which I have spoken. This dance is known generally in the American colonies by the name of Chica, which name it has in the Windward Islands and Saint Dominique.

When a Chica is to be danced several instruments will play a certain melody, which is devoted uniquely to this kind of dance, and in which the rhythm is strictly ob-

DANCE. 61

served. For the danseuse, who holds the corners of a handkerchief or the two ends of her apron, the art of this dance consists mainly in moving the lower part of the torso, while keeping the rest of the body almost motionless. To speed up the movement of the Chica, a dancer will approach his danseuse, throwing himself forward, almost touching her, withdrawing, then advancing again, while seeming to implore her to yield to the desires which invade them.

There is nothing lascivious or voluptuous which this tableau does not depict. It offers a kind of contest in which every trick of love and every means of triumph are displayed: fear, hope, disdain, tenderness, caprice, pleasure, denial, delirium, flight, intoxication, despair—and the followers of Pan surely would have celebrated the divinity of its inventor.

I find it difficult to note the impressions this dance produces, when it is precisely performed. It effects each look, it moves our sensibilities, fires our imagination; it even incites older people. I maintain that this magical idea could only originate in a sweet climate propitious to pleasure, and that it forms a monument indicative of the influence the dance can exert.

Not long ago the Chica was danced by beautiful young ladies whose simple graces embellished it and made it even more seductive. It is true they danced it alone or with members of their own sex who would take the role of the partner, without of course being quite as spectacular. Today, however, our customs are no longer pure enough for such an experiment. The Chica is no longer danced at the balls of the white ladies, and only occasionally is it performed on the spur of the moment at certain parties where the small and select society reassures the ladies.

The real style of the Chica is to be found among the negresses of the Dutch island of Curaçao, where it is difficult to imagine the degree to which they go to achieve the desired effects. They go so far that their breasts seem independent of their lower torsos, which they shake with an agility which is even tiring to the eyes.

The Chica comes to us from African lands, where it is danced by nearly every tribe, particularly in the Congo. The negroes brought it to the Antilles, where it soon was naturalized. Throughout the Spanish American continent the Chica held such universal sway that it was performed publicly in religious ceremonies and processions on Christmas Eve. Even nuns would perform in their convent courtyard, publicly executing the voluptuous steps of the Chica, expressing the joy they felt at the birth of the Christ who came to take away the sins of the world through his death.

America is not the only country to have felt this African influence, because the Moors who brought the passionate Fandango to Spain were in fact transporting the Chica which was only slightly less developed due to a difference of climate and various cultural factors.

It should be interesting to attempt to discover where the Chica originated. It has been attributed to the negroes of the Guinea Coast, though an important fact negates this—the nudity of these African peoples. Who does not know that nature loses, for people who go without clothes, the major part of the sweet pleasures? Where would we have found all the delightful nothings, all the degrees of desire, which are part of the Chica? What comparison could possibly be established, for instance, between the Chica and the action of the naked Carribeans from Saint Vincent Island, who taking each other by the arm, two by two, bend and rise for hours on end, while emitting a few lugubrious, monotonous tones, all the while believing they have been dancing? Perhaps the Caribbeans and the originators of the Chica had a love of the dance and the effects of climate in common, but what a difference in customs!

Almost without wishing it this observation reminds me of the unhappy natives of Saint Dominique, who had several historical dances, such as a Pyrrhic dance, and others as voluptuous as the Chica.

I know that they were unclothed, but history has revealed a sufficient number of facts for us to realize that originally the Indians of the four great islands of the Antilles came from the continent. Doubtless they had enough communication with more civilized peoples to realize that charms hidden from the curious often are more potent than those too generously displayed. This thought must have been present when their dances were invented, and, if the reproach of historians that these dances are lascivious is correct, we do not doubt that, as in the Chica, the excess lay in exposure, which prevented the delicate separation of voluptuousness from obscenity.

But the Carribean natives were themselves immigrants, having little idea of the nature of the dances of the Indians, whose implacable enemies they were. From whatever place they may have come before arriving in this area, certainly they knew no dances inspired by pleasure—their bloody customs would have frightened away pleasure.

Rather, is it not necessary to attribute this ingenious discovery to that country in which the fine arts and the purest taste have become immortal, to that country where it was said that Socrates, intoxicated by dancing, demonstrated to what extent the triumph of Aspasia could go? Greece had a temperate climate and was suited so that its inhabitants, who cultivated every form of sensual pleasure, were able to spread their compelling doctrines in both Asia and Africa. We know that in Asia the Persians have lively and amorous dances. In Egypt, on happy wedding days, do we not see dancers come to show the bride through pleasant pantomime the still-veiled mysteries which the God orders them to celebrate, and do not these dancers prepare the way to crown voluptuousness? It seems to me that the passion of all Asia Minor for these dances, tutored by love, has an analogy in the Chica, and, if Horace the troubadour of pleasure was obliged to censure the Ionian dance, I have already remarked that one could also censure the ecstasy to which the Chica leads on occasion.

I cannot defend myself from the prejudice that always leads me back to Greece, when I observe there was a Greek dance called the Candiote, depicting principally the story of Theseus and Ariadne; and meanwhile in Saint Dominique one says of an African or a negro Creole that he is Candiot if he is above all preoccupied with pleasure and love of the dance. Can it be coincidence which causes this similarity, and is chance so important that one may not seek the origin of the Chica among a people who have filled the universe with their glory, their celebrity in all activities, and above all their exquisite delicacy in all that breathes voluptuousness?

When one considers once more the dance of the Carribean natives from Saint Vincent, one will agree that the Chica could only have been created by those whose fiery imagination supplied that which one's eyes should not see.

F I N